1 MONTH OF
FREE
READING

at

www.ForgottenBooks.com

By purchasing this book you are eligible for one month membership to ForgottenBooks.com, giving you unlimited access to our entire collection of over 1,000,000 titles via our web site and mobile apps.

To claim your free month visit:

www.forgottenbooks.com/free781648

ISBN 978-0-428-77322-9
PIBN 10781648

This book is a reproduction of an important historical work. Forgotten Books uses
state-of-the-art technology to digitally reconstruct the work, preserving the original format
whilst repairing imperfections present in the aged copy. In rare cases, an imperfection in
the original, such as a blemish or missing page, may be replicated in our edition. We do,
however, repair the vast majority of imperfections successfully; any imperfections that
remain are intentionally left to preserve the state of such historical works.

IMPORTANT.

The New Register of the Institute is now in Press.

TITLE-PAGE AND NAMES OF COUNCILORS WILL BE AS SHOWN ON THE FOLLOWING PAGES, WITH THE EXCEPTION THAT NAMES WILL BE ARRANGED ALPHABETICALLY.

THE NAME OF EVERY COUNCILOR SHOULD APPEAR IN THIS PUBLICATION.

COUNCILORS WHO HAVE NOT FURNISHED THE NECESSARY INFORMATION ARE REQUESTED TO DO SO AT ONCE.

A blank form will be furnished for the purpose, upon application, addressed to

AMERICAN INSTITUTE OF CIVICS,

177 BROADWAY,

New York.

P 638

NATIONAL CORPS OF LECTURERS

AND

FACULTY ASSOCIATES IN HIGHER INSTITUTIONS OF LEARNING.

Councilors of the Institute who are willing to accept invitations to deliver occasional addresses on subjects related to Civics (affairs of government, citizenship, etc.), and who are not now enrolled as members of its Corps of Lecturers, and members of faculties in higher institutions of learning who are willing to co-operate with the Institute in its general activities, are invited to send information to this effect at once, in order that their names may be properly presented in the new Register.

Address

AMERICAN INSTITUTE OF CIVICS,

177 BROADWAY,

NEW YORK.

AMERICAN INSTITUTE OF CIVICS.

REGISTER

OF ITS

NATIONAL BODY OF COUNCILORS,

INCLUDING

FACULTY ASSOCIATES IN HIGHER INSTITUTIONS OF LEARNING

AND

NATIONAL CORPS OF LECTURERS.

A. D. 1900.

PUBLISHED BY

THE AMERICAN INSTITUTE OF CIVICS.

NEW YORK.

[OVER.]

COUNCILORS AMERICAN INSTITUTE OF CIVICS.

Foster, Capt. Herbert Sidney. U. S. In-
fantry. Manila, P. I.; Prof. Milit. Sc., etc., Univ.
Vt., 1890-3. Commander Vt. Div. S. of V.,
1891-2; Memb. S. A. R., S. V., M. O. L. L., Soc.
Army of Santiago de Cuba. B. Calais, Vt., Aug.
8, 1853.

Sanford, Fernando. Prof. Physics, Leland
Stanford Univ., Cal. Memb. Soc. Am. Wars.
B. Taylor, Ill., 1854.

Thompson, Hon. Hugh Smith. Comptrol-
ler N. Y. Life Ins. Co., 346 B'way, N. Y. City.
Capt. C. S. A., Civ. War; late Supt. Educ. and
Governor S. C.; Ass. Sec. U. S. Treas.; Civ.
Serv. Com. U. S.; Memb. S. R.; Confed. Vet.
Camp; South. Soc.; Ref. C.; Century Ass., N.
Y., and St. Andrew's Soc., Charleston, S. C.,
where b. 1836.

Beaver, Gen. James Addams, LL.D. Law,
Bellefonte, Pa. U. S. Civ. War, Lt. 2d Pa..
Lt.-Col. 45th Pa., Col. 148th Pa. and Bvt. Brig.-
Gen. U. S. V.; Gov. Pa. 1887-91.; Judge Super.
Ct. Pa. 1895; Memb. U. S. Com. on Conduct
Spanish War; Trust. Wash. & Jeff. Coll.,
Pa. State Coll., Lincoln Univ.; Memb. S. R.;
Milit. Ord. L. L.; U. V. Leg.; G. A. R.; Soc.
Army Potomac and West Va.; Pa. German
Soc.; U. L. Club, Philad.; B Θ Π Frat. B.
Millerstown, Pa., Oct. 21, 1837.

* Bonaparte, Charles Joseph. Law, Balti-
more, Md. Overseer Harvard Univ.; Trust.
Pratt Free Library, Balt.; Memb. Nat. Civ.
Serv. Ref. Ass.; Balt. Charity Org. Soc.; Nat.
Munic. League, etc. B. Balt., Md., June 9, 1851.

Riggs, Rev. Thomas Lawrence. Supt. In-
dian Missions, Oahu, S. D. B. Lacquiparle.
Minn., June 3, 1847.

McConnell, John Preston, A.M. Chair
Latin & Greek, Milligan College, Milligan, Tenn.
Memb. Am. Acad. Polit. & Soc. Science; & Am.
Hist. Assoc. B. Wayland, Va., Feb. 22, 1866.

* Cruikshank, James, LL.D. 206 So. Oxford
St., Brooklyn, N. Y. Princ. Gram. Sch. No. 12, &
Eve. High. Sch., Brooklyn; Life Memb. Fellow,
& Secy. Council. Brooklyn Inst. of Arts &
Sciences; Assoc. Sup. Pub. Schools. Bklyn.,
1866-72; Ed. N. Y. Teacher, 1856-58; Institute
Lecturer. B. Argyle, N. Y., Aug. 28, 1831.

Symmes, Frank Jameson. 725 Mission St.,
San Francisco. Merchant; Director Mer-
chants' Assn.; Ex-Naval Officer ; Ex-Pres.
Harvard Club; Memb. University Club; V.-
P. Settlement Assoc., San Francisco; Also
Memb. Naval Bd. Visitors, 1899 & Soc. Am.
Wars. B. Kingston, Mass., June 7, 1847.

*Comstock, Theodore Bryant, Sc.D. Cornell.
Chicago, Ill., 535 Stimpson Block. Mining En-
gineer; Chair Geology Cornell Univ., 1875-79;
Chair Mining Engineering, Univ. Ill., 1885-89;
Director Sch. of Mines, Univ. of Arizona, 1891-
95; Pres. do., 1893-95; Founder & Fellow Geolog.
Soc. America; Memb. Natl. Geog. Soc., Fellow
Am. Soc. Adv. Sc.; Memb. Am. Inst. M. E., &
Federated Inst. of Eng. Societies, England. B.
Cuyahoga Falls, N. Y., July 27, 1849.

Sherman, Hon. Elijah B., LL.D. Chicago,
Ill., 1152 Monadnock Bldg. Lawyer & Master
in Chancery U. S. Cir. Court; Lt. Co. C. 9th
Vt. Inf. Civ. War; Lt.-Col. & Judge Adv. 1st
Brig. N. G. Ill., 1877-84; Memb. Ill. Legis.

1877-81; G. M. I. O. O. F. Ill. 1874; Memb. G.
A. R.; LL.; Vet. Union; U. L. Club, Chicago;
Ill. Bar Assoc. & Am. Bar Assoc., and National
Pres. Delta Upsilon Fraternity. B. Fairfield, Vt.,
Jun. 18, 1832.

Conant, Hon. Edward, A.M. Princ. Pub.
School, Randolph, Vt.; State Supt. Education,
Vt., 1874-80; Memb. Const. Conv. Vt., 1870;
Delegate National Council Cong. Churches,
1865-74-92; Internat. Ditto, 1899; Author Hist.
Vt.; Drill Book in English Primary Hist.
Reader. B. Pomfret, Vt., May 10, 1829.

†Hamilton, Rev. W. E., D.D. Chair of Phi-
losophy & Civics in Simpson College, Indian-
ola, Ia. B. New Richmond, O., Oct. 9, 1845.

Jefferson, John Percival. Manufacturer,
Warren, Pa.; Lieutenant U. S. Army (West
Point). B. Delaware, O., 1852.

Trafton, William Henry. Editor & Statis-
tician, 210 W. 83d St., New York City, Memb.
Produce Exchange, Press Association, & West
Side Repub. Club, New York.

Breckenridge, Gen. Joseph Cabell. Wash-
ington, D. C., War Dept. Brig. Gen. & In-
spect. Gen. U. S. A.; Maj. Gen. U. S. Vols.
Span. Am. War Memb. S. A. R.; L. L.; Mil.
Ord. Foreign Wars; Ord. Span. Am. War;
Soc. Army Cumberland, & Tenn.; Trustee Am.
Inst. Civics. B. Baltimore, Md., May 14, 1842.

Spayd, H. H. Minersville, Pa. Prin. Pub.
Schools; Color Bearer 149th Pa. Vols. Civ.
War; Licentiate Eng. Bap. Ch.; Memb. G. A.
R.; Life Memb. Pa. State Teachers' Ass. &
Nat. Ed. Ass. B. Myerstown, Pa., Oct. 26, 1845.

Kingsbury, Frederick John. Waterbury,
Ct., Banker. Memb. Yale Univ. Corporation,
1881, 1900; Treas. P. E. Diocese of Ct?, & trustee
various Educ. & Charitable bodies; Memb.
Soc. Col. Wars; Ct. Acad. Sc.; Am. Antiq.
Soc.; Am. Soc. Sc. Ass.; Am. Hist. Soc., and
Am. Archeolog. Soc. B. Waterbury, Ct.

†Howard, Hon. Walter E., LL.D. Middle-
bury, Vt., Lawyer. Chair Polit. Sc. & Hist.,
Middlebury College since 1889. Ex-Senator
& Rep. State of Vt.; Ex.-Memb. U. S. Consular
Service, and Pres. Vt. Bd. Norm. Sch. Com-
missioners. B. Tunbridge, Vt., May 29, 1849.

†Reed, Rev. George Edward, S.T.D., LL.D.
Carlisle, Pa. Pres. Dickinson College; Libra-
rian Pa. State Library; Former pastor leading
churches N. Y. E. Conf. M. E. Ch. B. Brown-
ville, Me., Mch. 28, 1846.

*Logan, Walter Seth. 27 William St., New
York City, Lawyer. Grad. Yale Univ. 1870;
Memb. Am. Bar Ass., and Pres. N. Y. State Bar
Ass.; Memb. Ord. Founders & Patriots; Colon.
Wars; S. A. R.; N. E. Soc.; a liberal patron
Arts & Sciences, & popular speaker on Hist. &
Economical subjects. B. Washington, Ct.,
Apr. 15, 1847.

*Crocker, Hon. George Glover, LL.B.
(Harv.). Boston, Mass., 19 Milk St., Lawyer.
Pres. Mass. Senate 1883; Chairman Mass. Bd.
R. R. Comrs., 1887-92; Chairman Boston Transit
Commission, since 1894; Author "Principles
of Procedure in Delib. Bodies;" G. P. Putnam's
Sons. B. Boston, Dec. 15, 1843.

---

* Member National Corps of Lecturers.   † Member Faculty Associates.   (OVER.)

DIPLOMATIC SERVICE AND ITS REQUIREMENTS.

By Hon. Geo. F. Seward, former U. S. Minister to China.

There is no diplomatic service of the United States. There is a diplomatic establishment. The Government appoints Ministers from time to time to given parts. These appointments are made from the ranks of our citizenship, but not from a body of men constituting a service.

The European Governments select young men for their diplomatic services, assigning them to duty first in their foreign offices or legations and promoting them step by step for merit. In other words, they adhere practically to the methods which we follow in our Naval and Military services. Our plan permits each President to name whomsoever he pleases for the highest as well as the lowest places, the choice being made usually without regard to prior service.

There has been no time in the whole history of our country when we have not had some men serving us abroad qualified in a high degree for their duties. We have such men to-day. Mr. Andrew D. White and Mr. Strauss have served under different administrations and may be considered trained diplomatic officers. Their appointments indicate recognition of the fact that experience in diplomacy is valuable. We have also in the establishment at the moment Mr. Joseph H. Choate and General Porter. The native ability and the breadth of general experience of these men stand in place of special training.

Beyond a doubt men of ability may always be found ready to take service abroad. Sometimes they are attracted by the honor which attaches to the duty. Sometimes they are weary of work at home and are seeking rest. Sometimes they find in a foreign post opportunities for study. It is nevertheless safe to say that nine out of every ten persons in our diplomatic service, so called, have been chosen, not for fitness, but for political reasons. This one was active in politics, that one was related to someone active in politics, another was in the way of someone active in politics, that one failed of an election while carrying the party banner and must be provided for, another subscribed heavily for the party's campaign treasury and so on.

This haphazard system or lack of system is followed when surely the need of a right system is great. It is not a light thing to be the person selected to make public appearance for our nation at the capital of some other great nation, to mingle with its statesmen in representative capacity, to speak on great occasions and to take part in great public functions. But the social and ceremonial duties of a diplomat are incidental only to his graver duties. There are no international Courts in which international controversies, grave or unimportant, can be tried. There is no power resident in an international agent to demand, to threaten or to use force. He is limited to such influence as his representative capacity and his personal qualities afford. And upon these he must rely to win over the Government to which he is accredited to the wishes and purposes of his own Government.

Again, to be the dependable source of information for the foreign office of one's State is by itself not a light thing. It is difficult for most men to take just views of home questions. It is far away more difficult to judge of questions in a foreign state. It is not merely the case that to get at facts is not an easy task when one is amid a strange people. The facts must be considered and presented with knowledge of local institutions, methods of administration and national idiosyncrasies. The presentation must be absolutely without prejudice. The natural instinct of every man is to believe the morals and the methods, the manners and the fashions of his own country the best, and all morals, methods, manners and fashions which are different, ridiculous if not vicious. All this points to the proposition that a diplomatic agent must be capable of entering into the spirit of the people with whom he lives, of appreciating their institutions and of judging them by their own standards.

We all know that success in any line of individual effort does not necessarily indicate breadth of ability. The successful lawyer may be a special pleader, the successful preacher a bigot, the successful merchant may know little beside cotton goods or coffee. But the successful diplomat must be many-sided, accomplished, shrewd, free from prejudices, appreciative and just. He must know what is serious (and that is a serious thing indeed). He must know also how to fit means to ends. He must be a man of character, absolutely honest and absolutely incapable of misleading his own Government or that to which he is accredited.

I am quite aware that many people estimate the quality of a diplomat differently. In their estimation his proper function is often to make the wrong side appear the better, to speak speciously rather than sincerely. Will the man of character do these things ever? Will the man who does such things be acceptable to men of character in the State he represents or in that to which he is accredited? It is only necessary to state the question to enforce the conclusion. If high character is needed anywhere it is needed in diplomacy if permanent success is to be achieved.

To any right statement of the qualities of a diplomat there must be included this proposition—he must be unselfish. There is a saying that "Peace hath her victories no less renowned than war." But a saying quite as true would be, "Peace hath her victories which are not renowned at all." The victories of a diplomatic agent are generally such. If he heralds them to the world he destroys his usefulness. Perhaps the hardest of all tasks for an American politician turned diplomat is to hold his tongue about his achievements, real or fancied.

Again, no man probably ever became the spokesman of any nation or of any interest who did not feel the task of moderating and managing his own side greater than of managing the other. Stewart L. Woodford is said to have declared that if left alone he would have averted war with Spain while gaining for Cuba all that America could reasonably desire. The instance is salient, but it illustrates my point. No Secretary of State is gifted with universal knowledge or universal sagacity; neither is any President or Cabinet. The nation's representative abroad is, so to speak, casting the line and taking the soundings. If well informed, he is able to chart the course to be pursued. A foreign secretary without able representatives in foreign States is in a very helpless position.

A concrete instance of the highest type of a diplomat is Benjamin Franklin. Whether one considers his accomplishments, his common sense, his shrewdness, his constancy, his balance of judgment, his personal charm, his acquaintance with affairs and human nature, his freedom from prejudices, no man was ever better qualified to win respect and to achieve success.   If you will keep him in mind as the ideal representative of what the foreign representative of a government should be you will at least know of what my conception of that ideal is.

The clash of interests between the European States is such that greater importance attaches to their foreign services than is the case with us.   It is Cavour, Bismarck and Disraeli, the men of their day in their respective States, who deal with foreign affairs.   But even with us the post of Secretary of State is the leading one, and it is true that the line of Secretaries of State has been more distinguished for ability and the general qualities of statesmanship than the line of our Presidents.

Our Government is based upon moral ideas.   It is just these ideas which may be enforced in diplomacy.   When the conclusions of a government may be enforced by arms, when the State is great because of its military resources, diplomacy is of less importance.   Brute force instead of moral power is at the front.   A late representative of our nation in Asia has said that before the victory of Dewey he sat helplessly in his seat, his hands hanging by his side. Was that man aware of the moral weight of his country?   Had he learned the alphabet even of his profession?   Burlingame once represented America at that same Court.   It was in the dark days of our Civil War and no one of our men-of-war was on that side of the globe.   Perhaps no diplomatic agent of any nation was ever more respected at that Court or more successful than he.

I mention the instance of our helpless representative, not to throw a stone, but to illustrate a proposition.   Our nation is as ignorant almost of the use which may be made of its diplomatic establishment as the given Minister was of the possibilities of his position.   I have quoted Mr. Woodford's claim that he could have settled the Cuban issue satisfactorily.   Our nation was so little acquainted with the idea that great issues may be settled by diplomacy that it drifted into war.   Do we, as a nation, appreciate the moral weight of our country?   For America there should never be need of war.   We ought never to embark upon any wrong adventure.   If right in the issue our strength is such that no exhibition of it should be necessary.   As a matter of fact, however, we have never learned how little we need to anticipate war nor how to build and use a diplomatic establishment which may serve to avert it.

If regard be had only to issues of peace or war it must be remembered that these have come to us of late with alarming frequency.   In ten years we have had a grave dispute with Chili over the abuse of sailors, with England over the Venezuelan boundary matter, and with Spain over Cuba.   The two former were settled.   The latter resulted in a war which has led to a second war, the end of which is not yet in sight.   Diplomacy which would have averted these wars would have been cheap at any imaginable cost.   But outside of issues involving war or peace it would be difficult to overestimate the duties of a diplomatic agent.   In a thousand ways he may be useful to his country and his countrymen. In whatever case his State or people touch the State or people to which he is accredited, his services may be needed. He has a guardianship as respects the private rights of individuals of his nationality and as respects the rights of the commonwealth. He prepares treaties and he enforces the observance of them. He studies and reports upon administrative matters. He watches the course of scientific discoveries and points the way to the utilization of them at home. He is expected to be broadly useful and the variety and extent of his work is such that he has the fullest opportunities for the exercise of the highest qualities and accomplishments.

Surely when such is the case we might properly suppose that our Government has fitted means to ends in providing an efficient and creditable diplomatic establishment. Our failure to do so is extreme.

In the first place we do not pay our representatives adequately. This will be evident on the slightest presentation of the facts.

There are six Ambassadors in the service. The highest salary paid is $17,500, the lowest $12,000.

Note how this compares with the salaries of men in business employments, railroad presidents, for instance. The latter are paid from $30,000 to $60,000 a year. The aggregate sum paid to six Ambassadors would only pay the salary of the president of a first-class railway one and a half times.

There are twenty-four Ministers Plenipotentiary. These receive in the aggregate $213,000, or about $9,000 each, or individually, say, one-sixth of the salary of a railway president.

There are four Ministers Resident receiving altogether $19,000, or less than $5,000 each.

Considering that a foreign representative must live in a style befitting his capacity as an international agent, does it not seem absurd to pay him, not merely on a lower scale than a business man of high grade, but actually less than competent salesmen in wholesale stores sometimes receive.

In the next place a Minister's official residence should be dignified as suited to his station. With us it is such, in fact, as the given representative is disposed or can afford to make it. This obviously is wrong. The Government should own an official house at each capital and it should be on a suitable scale. Our foreign representatives are often lodged so cheaply that they suffer in public estimation.

Again, a foreign representative should be well equipped for his work. He should speak the language of the Court to which he is accredited or at least should speak French, which measurably is the language of diplomacy. He should be thoroughly familiar with international law and with the forms and usages of diplomatic representation. When so equipped he is just fitted to begin the delicate duty devolved upon him. Years of experience will be required to make him a diplomat in the sense that the men trained in the European services are diplomats. The rudiments of his profession well acquired will not make him a diplomat in a right sense any more than study in the law school or medical college will make a man fit to be employed for work in the trial of cases or the curing of diseases. Actual work in his proper field will be as necessary to his success as it is in the success of men in other vocations. For one lawyer of the stamp of Webster or Choate, there are thousands who live from hand to mouth. We do not always stop to consider that men able to command success in two or more diverse occupations are far away fewer. in proportion. A man is like a tool. He has fitness when trained for one thing. He cannot readily be made over to fitness for another thing. We Americans consider ourselves more adaptable than other peoples. We also think ourselves more virtuous. Perhaps we are, but perhaps also we are more vain. "Vanity of vanities," saith the preacher.

Americans touch government most closely in the administration of local municipalities.. He would be a bold American who would declare that there is very much virtue or capacity exhibited in the control of our cities. We touch our diplomatic establishment the least of all our departments. He may be a bold American who supposes we are reasonably successful in it. We cannot take our diplomatic establishment and, so to speak, weigh it in a balance and compare weights with those of other nations. The success of an individual is due to qualities which are equally incapable of being measured. Even personal charms are of an intangible sort. The eye of the poet rolls in a fine frenzy, but an eye habitually rolling in frenzy does not make its owner a poet. It is an old saying that you may vote that a horse shall be a general, but that does not make him so.

The success of our diplomatic establishment at large must be derived from the success of its individual members. If it is to stand high, if the weight is to be right, the units must be right. If we are to have a right weight of units we must choose them on a right system. And there is no way in private business or in public to be reasonably sure of the merit of any choice of an agent which is not determined from observation of the fitness of the individual in the same line of duty. Until men have proven themselves right diplomats, there is no certainty that they will do diplomatic work well. Until we have a diplomatic service in which each individual may be tested, we will have no way to choose our units with any certainty of being right.

Is this all theory? I grant it. Is it a reasonable theory? Each must judge for himself or herself. Having so judged, then rack your brains and answer also whether any system which is not right in theory works out well in practice. My own experience is that we might as well try to make water run up hill by gravity as to try to make a success in working any business on wrong lines. One may be a theorist and fail. One cannot be a successful administrator unless consciously or unconsciously he follows a system based on right theory.

We may distrust the theory of any European State. We may distrust any theory adhered to by all the European States. They all adhere to the idea that a diplomatic establishment must be operated as a service. There diplomatic work is important. The great State has great interests. The small State must conserve and safeguard what it has. Do you find in the practice of the dozen or more European States—this uniform practice of all—any defense for the American system? If you do I will take off my hat metaphorically in presence of your sturdy patriotism and just keep on wondering whether your patriotic hats have unduly compressed the gray matter under them.

I will not undertake to develop the details of the service system as practiced in Europe. I may say that it involves the careful choice of the novices. They must be persons who have won their spurs in the universities. Formerly they had to come from families habituated to the service of the State. We have university men also, and it is by no means difficult with us to find also persons who have had relations in office. The race of Plunketts, of Murphys, even the stock of Crokers, may not soon die out. So far as this goes we have a broader supply, perhaps, of the raw material for diplomacy than any European power, it may be than all combined.

Of the ways of culling men for advancement or the reverse practiced in Europe I shall not speak. Seniority is no more the rule for promotions than it was in our Navy in the last war. Incapacity, too, finds its level sooner in a regular service.

There is one pertinent question about the service plan. Will it have members enough to develop the best results? Will there be room for choice? Europe has found no reason to hesitate on this score. America probably would not. It has always seemed to be, however, that it would be well for us to make the consular establishment also a service and to permit of the choice of diplomatic agents from the lists of both services. There are ten Consuls for one Minister, and the training in each branch is largely similar.

I am well aware of the failing of human kind which leads people to consider what is as best. I am well aware that a reformer is generally considered an unpractical schemer. There is no use in finding fault with this tendency of human nature. I am fain to believe, however, that the American people are honestly striving for the things which are best. I have no desire to put before you anything excepting my conception of what is best. With the question whether the best thing as I conceive it is going to be adopted I am not concerned at the moment. I did not come to you to make prophecies. But I may say this that the thing which is logical and right will come to pass sooner or later unless, indeed, the American state tends to the worse rather than to the better things.

It is quite true that a vicious system tends to develop on its vicious side. It is also true that when any system has gone very bad remedial measures are likely to be taken. Our system has not yet shown up so badly that the call for a change has become loud. But undoubtedly it is becoming worse. With the machine politicians controlling all nominations to public office, with our Presidents consulting machine bosses and deferring to them in all ways, what chance is there that our foreign ministers will be chosen for merit. Joseph H. Choate could not be selected Minister to England until the Republican boss of New York had been consulted. Merit is in fact the last thing which is considered. · Machine politics are everywhere. It is an era of degradation in our public services. It is an era which may be succeeded by a better one. A similar or worse degradation of the public services existed in Great Britain, but better things have come there. When we get beyond machine politics, when the people come to their own, we will get not one, but many, reforms. Until then all reform movements will lag.

THE CENTRALIZATION OF POPULATION AS AFFECTING THE FUTURE OF DEMOCRACY.

By Adna F. Weber, Ph. D., Deputy Commissioner of Labor Statistics, State of New York.

For many years the portentous growth of our great cities has perturbed the thoughts of American statesmen and publicists, who believe, like their European rivals, that the strength of a nation rests upon the vigor and enterprise of the cultivators of the soil. "God made the country; man made the city." The gradual but persistent transformation of our country from a community of land owners into a nation of city-dwellers is one of the most striking social phenomena of the century. The United States has to-day a single city numbering more inhabitants than could be counted in the whole country 100 years ago. *Then* there were only five American towns with a population of 10,000 or more, and the greatest of these was no larger than Yonkers or Long Island City. *Then* not one American in thirty was a town-dweller; to-day, every third American you meet has his home in a city (a town of 8,000 or more inhabitants). And at the present rate of change, it will be only one or two decades more before one-half the inhabitants of this country are city people.

Let it not be thought that this momentous movement of population is the consequence of conditions peculiar to our own country. On the contrary, the same phenomenon appears throughout the old and settled communities of Europe. Leaving out of consideration the newly built cities of the West, brought into being by the swift occupation of that unopened empire, the observer will soon recognize that city for city, old Europe equals or surpasses young America. In the last half century Berlin has grown more rapidly than the metropolitan district of New York, including Brooklyn and the Jersey cities; Vienna has distanced Philadelphia; Hamburg, Boston; and Buda-Pesth, Baltimore. In the other countries of Europe cities have been growing up at a rate scarcely less rapid.

In Europe, too, the concentration of population is more extreme than in the United States. At least twelve other countries have a larger percentage of urbanites, defining the city as a place of 10,000 population. If the comparison be restricted to large cities (those of 100,000 or more inhabitants), the United States will rank about tenth among the nations in respect to centralization of its population. In England two-thirds of the people are now town-dwellers, while one-third dwell in great cities. Likewise in Scotland, Australia and Uruguay one-third of the people are residents of cities of 100,000. In the United States as a whole the percentage of population resident in such great cities is only 15.5, or one in six; but in individual states this percentage is greatly exceeded. Thus, one-half of the people of New York State confess allegiance to the metropolis alone and another large fraction dwell in Buffalo, Rochester, Syracuse and the two Hudson River towns.

The causes of such a universal centralization of population in the present century are not deeply hidden. Until the opening of this century, few of the large cities of the world could have continued their existence if cut off from the country, for they lost more by deaths than they gained in births and depended on the rural districts for recruits. The progress of medical science and of public sanitation has however stayed the ravages of death, so that at the present time the cities enjoy a large excess of births over deaths. This *natural* increase alone would explain the accelerated growth of cities in recent times. But why does the current of migration from farm and village to city, once so essential to the city's existence, still move onward in undiminished volume, after the city has demonstrated its ability to supply its own increase? The answer is given by the laws of industry and economics. The centralization of population is simply a phase of the evolution of society.

Many Americans, even here in the East, can remember the day when their parents not only tilled the soil, but produced their own wool, spun and wove their own clothes, and had their boots made by the village shoemaker. The widening of the social bond has changed all that. The factory and the railroad, mutual allies and friends, have taken away from the tillers of the soil all subsidiary occupations and removed them to the city. The miller, the weaver, the shoemaker, the cabinet maker have all moved to town. And this transfer of industries from the country to the city is going on to-day. To-morrow men now at work harvesting or plowing on the farm will be called to the city to make the machinery that will in future plow the fields and harvest the grain.

The cities are centers of industry and commerce, and as both industry and commerce are always rapidly increasing, while agriculture increases but slowly in obedience to the gradual growth of population, it follows that the cities must continue to absorb an increasing proportion of people.

The movement of population from the country to the city is attended with certain dangers weich have been frequently proclaimed. The most obvious of these dangers is a deterioration in the physique or morals of the people, brought about by the overcrowded conditions of city life, the lack of pure air and wholesome exercise. A review of the recent vital statistics, however, shows that the death rate of the great cities is being steadily reduced. In one of two of the German States, indeed, the cities are now actually more healthy than the rural districts. Less progress has been made in this country, so far as can be judged, from our imperfect vital statistics; and it is very necessary that the work of reform be undertaken with renewed vigor. We need additional small parks and playgrounds (the lungs of the great city), more stringent building laws and their honest enforcement, and especially more rapid transit, so as to permit working people to move out of crowded tenements to cottage homes on the outskirts.

Another problem that we shall have to solve is imposed upon us by the concentration of wealth accompanying the concentration of population. So long as wealth is honestly used, the American people are not disposed to debate the expediency of private ownership. But when the possessors of natural monopolies like gas, water, electric lighting and street railways enter into an alliance with the people's representatives for the purpose of exploiting the citizen, then there arises a disposition to question the wisdom of private ownership and management. We cannot blind our eyes to the fact that the policy of public control of quasi-public undertakings has so far failed in this country as to provoke a strong agitation in favor of socialism. If socialism is the only remedy left, it is by all means preferable that the first experiments be made in small communities before the State and the nation are called upon to embark upon such a venturesome policy.

In still another direction can the cities be of service to democracy, namely, in preserving the open competition which our ideals regard as essential in the process of natural selection. The fundamental social problem is how to bring capable men to the front; to put the true social leaders in positions of responsibility. In countries where a system of caste prevails, the function of providing leaders is exercised by the aristocracy; and in such countries the need of great arenas or meeting grounds of talent is not felt. But a democracy of such territorial extent as our own requires *foci* of competition as the central instruments of natural selection. Such *foci* are, in fact, our great cities, and the social service which they render is of incalculable value.

THE PROBLEM OF CHARITY.

By Edward T. De Vine, Ph. D., Secretary Charity Organization Society, New York.

I trust, and have some grounds for believing, that the problem of charity in its narrower sense is of diminishing importance. By charity in its narrower sense, I mean, of course, that charity which seeks expression in material gifts—of money or kind—the necessity for which arises from some deficiency, either of will or of capacity in the one who receives them. The spirit of humanity has grown ever stronger, more sensitive, more dominating. In no civilized community does it now tolerate obvious suffering from the lack of food, shelter, clothing, medical care, nor in children does it permit an entire absence of educational opportunities, or of other necessary social conditions of normal development. Organized charity, using that expression as a collective term for relief societies, hospitals, asylums, nurseries, and other established agencies for the relief and prevention of distress, is a different and, whatever its occasional critics may say, a better thing than the spasmodic, ineffectual and ill-distributed personal charity from which it sprang. It is the unknown term in the earlier problem of charity which has been found and which, to use still the language of algebra, we may now substitute to our great advantage in the larger but perhaps, after all, the simpler problem of which we still seek the solution. To the uninitiated it looks like dubious progress to substitute for the simple symbol of an unknown quantity the elaborate and complicated expression in which at a certain stage the known factors insist upon disguising themselves. Even so, there are those who inveigh against present institutionalism in charity and lament the passing of simpler arrangements by which in a primitive society help is given to neighbors. Be patient. Our social progress will unfold in time, from these complicated and as yet too mechanical institutions and agencies, a system which shall have one present completeness and vastness, a symmetrical plan for meeting all types of distress, and for anticipating all possible physical disasters, while satisfying better perhaps than at present our legitimate demands for a better adaptation of institutions to varying and irreducible human nature.

In the practice of charity we generalize too quickly. We form unwarranted conclusions from one or two personal experiences, or, still worse, we take them ready-made without any experiences at all. We have known, it may be, of some striking instance of undeserved and unavoidable misfortune. Illness, or a relative's death, or business reverses, or an industrial displacement such as sometimes occurs, has left some friend of ours stranded. We have known of the family stock from which he sprang. We have known his industry, his prudence in ordinary matters, his integrity. Without thinking of the matter at any great length, without investigation, of course, for we have known the facts, with a promptness and spontaneity which do credit to both head and heart, we spring to his assistance, help him over his temporary embarrassment, place him under obligations which, since they are but an incident in a lifelong friendship, are justly ignored upon both sides. Help that helps has been given and not help that harms, and no harm has come of it. Outside of the friends concerned, no one knows of the transaction at all. This experience is not uncommon, but it is an uncommonly dangerous one from which to generalize in the adoption of a line of action which falls to any extent outside the conditions suggested.

The difficulties in which those are involved who ask help from strangers, or from persons who are richer in the possession of worldly goods than themselves are not often primarily due to causes outside themselves. They are due either to faults which must be eradicated, or, as I think more often, to the absence of qualities, moral or economic, which they and their children must develop unless the dependency is to be permanent. If we are unwilling to contribute to the dependency and weakness of our neighbors whom we do not know personally, we shall not give that which supplies their present apparent needs, creating in them expectations which we do not intend to fulfill, causing them it may be to sink to a lower level still in appeals to others, even for the things which, when we gave to them, they were earning for themselves. Such dependency is progressive and rapid. We are in danger of creating it whenever, without knowledge or reflection, we give in alms that which is asked of us, whether it be money, or clothes or food, or drink. There is another generalization of an opposite sort to which under modern conditions the average citizen is even more prone.

He finds that some case of destitution which has especially appealed to him is fraudulent. He gets a very unfavorable report from the investigating society to which he has referred it. The man drinks, the children whose pinched and miserable faces had so drawn upon his pity are borrowed for purposes of begging, the pitiful letter to which he came so near responding with a generous check is one of a thousand sent out to names selected from the Elite Directory. The reaction from the benevolent glow to disappointment and disgust carries the victim to very unjust and unwarranted inferences. He grasps at the suggestion that charity is a vanity and a snare, and that there is no need to help others. He becomes callous and indifferent and thinks that he does his full duty if he sends an annual check to some charity society, and that he will be charitable henceforth by proxy.

Believe me, neither of these two opposite classes have so much as seen what the problem of charity really is. The view which I would present forbids the charitable from acting upon either of these easy generalizations.

I said that those who are obliged to ask for help are often without qualities which must be implanted or developed from latent germs. This does not at all necessarily involve any personal condemnation. Those who do not succeed in life may be persons of very attractive qualities. A clergyman preaching from the text, "Jacob have I loved, but Esau have I hated," contrasted the personal qualities of these two ancient Hebrews very much to Esau's advantage, but then pointed out that for God's immediate purposes Jacob did have the qualities which made him usable in the working out of the great plan of human history, and that Esau, lacking these, although as manly, magnanimous and truthful as his brother, was cowardly, parsimonious and crafty, yet went to the wall.

Now, the man who is in position to give relief has not the *rôle* of a moral judge. He is not expected to give as a righteous rewarder of virtue and punisher of vice. He is not called upon to decide, as the unwise nomenclature sometimes used in charity offices puts it, between the worthy and the unworthy. He does not say to himself, at least he ought not to say: I will give to this beggar because I like him, while I will turn my back upon that one because he seems to me to be a villain. Relief given upon this basis has no claim to be called charity. It has no real relation to the welfare of the recipient of the gift.

If, however, having abandoned absolutely the fruitless attempt to adjust his alms in some way to the personal deserts of the beneficiary, the would-be benefactor takes into account the probable effect of his gifts, and if he selects his poor upon the principle that he will give only to those who may receive without injury, there open up before him at once the real problems, the fascinating problems of charity, the more modest but more fruitful problems at which hundreds of devoted men and women are working at this moment, to the solution of which I would invite yet hundreds more.

Do not think of our problem as one big, burning, baffling question to which an answer once for all can be found—Single Tax, eight hours or Socialism. It requires a long series of scientific experiments, accurately observed and recorded, cautious generalization, judicious comparison, patient investigation. Some light we have already.

For example, widows with small children may be liberally aided through some pension plan, by which rent and perhaps some other expenses are regularly paid. Even if an income large enough to meet all expenses is provided, they still have their full natural burden of caring for home and children. They are not pauperized by the provision of such an income. Dependent to an extent they are naturally and must be if they are to do their duty by their own children. This is a better form of assistance than to remove the children to an asylum, leaving the mother to earn her living as an unmarried woman might. It is better for the mother to have the task of caring for her own offspring. It is better for them to have the family influences and ties. It is cheaper for the community. So much may be said to be established, but there is even in this particular class of cases still much to be ascertained. From what source should this aid come? First of all, of course from near relatives. But when this fails? From the church if there are church ties?—from a benefit fund to which the husband had paid in dues?—from neighbors, from relief societies organized for this purpose, from strangers whom some society makes it a part of its business to interest?—from the public treasury? The one point about the matter on which nearly all thoughtful persons who have considered the matter are united, is that it should not be from the public treasury. About all else we are in a stage of investigation and discussion and experiment.

Again, there is pretty general approval of whatever can be done either by private charity or from funds raised by taxation to cure disease, to prevent its spread, and to create favorable hygienic conditions. Where, however, is the line which separates in this field the duty of the State from that of private charity? Here lies a most interesting, and in this State at the present moment a most live and important theoretical problem. Shall we establish, as Massachusetts has just done, a State Sanatorium for incipient cases of pulmonary tuberculosis, and so attempt to check the ravages of the great white plague about which we have learned so much within a dozen years, but without as yet, as Dr. Pryor, of Buffalo, said recently at the Academy of Medicine, having utilized our knowledge in such a way as to benefit in the slightest degree the great body of the suffering poor whom it ravages as neither war nor all other human diseases combined harass them. It is a live question, with which in one form or another every State must grapple if it would not do violence to the very spirit of charity.

The problem of charity, put generally, is to enlist for the service of our common humanity the more thoughtful and continuous attention of good citizens in the tasks which fall upon the public and private charitable agencies in the community, to the end that public officials may have our intelligent criticism, our hearty support in the performance of their duty, our appreciation of their reforms and advances, our denunciation if they are recreant; and to the end that our private societies, religious and secular, charitable and educational, those that are highly organized, and those that are modest and largely individual in their plan, whatever their character and scope, may all be infused with a spirit of brotherhood, that they may be flexible, elastic, responsive to new needs, that they may be fit instruments in the hands of Providence for the regeneration of man and the creation of a new social order.

That the present discussion may be left in a concrete form it may be in place to point out certain charitable needs of our community at the present time. There are needed homes for aged persons in which those who are left homeless and friendless in old age, but whose lives have been decent, and who, because of good character, should be kept, if possible, from the almshouse. We have many such homes, but nearly all have long waiting lists, and in many instances those who are otherwise suitable candidates for admission to them are debarred because there are no vacancies, or because of strict rules requiring adhesion to a particular religious faith.

Homes for incurables and for convalescents are also unable to cope with the demand for their shelter. In certain districts day nurseries are needed with careful supervision to prevent their improper use and their unwise location. An increased number of sick diet kitchens would be justified. Increased relief funds that are available, not merely for supplying the bare necessities of life, but for expenditure in a given case, if necessary, in liberal amount, to provide for the entire maintenance of a family for brief periods under exceptional circumstances; a plan by which rent and other necessary recurring expenses may be met for a widow with several small children who is not in position, both to care for the children and to earn their support; institutions for the isolation of advanced cases of consumption, and also for the treatment of incipient cases —all these are needed. Most of all there is demanded an increase in the number of persons who are willing to give personal attention to families with whom they can become acquainted, and whom through a long period of years, if necessary, they can befriend.

THE BENEFITS AND DISADVANTAGES OF WOMAN'S ENTRANCE UPON MAN'S OCCUPATIONS.

By Mrs. Henry M. Sanders, Pres. League for Political Education, New York.

An occupation belongs to the person who can efficiently work at it without regard to sex. Man's occupation ? Who made them his ? True, in this country he has long enjoyed a monopoly, due to custom and tradition only, and not to the eternal fitness of things. It is not many decades since man's occupations were supposed to embrace every kind of work except housekeeping, nursing, and perhaps elementary teaching. Now women have shown that they can do as good work as men, in law, medicine, high schools and colleges, literature, painting, store-keeping, journalism, and in numerous branches of manufacturing, such as printing, bookbinding, pen-making, baking and agriculture. No occupation can be declared to be man's and man's alone, until women through many generations have had free opportunity to engage in it, and have finally failed in it. The list of their industrial achievements is continually growing.

In Chicago there are three women who intend to be satisfied with their new house. They have not only planned it according to their own ideas of the eternal fitness of a house, but are building it themselves. It is said that they have gone about it in a masterful way, with no heed to the crowds of spectators who line the sidewalks during working hours. The house is of brick, and the timbers for the framework were sawed and jointed and nailed without masculine aid. The daughters act as hod-carriers, and supply the mother, who is chief bricklayer, with mortar and brick.

These three women are demonstrating the capacity of their sex for several trades which custom has hitherto precluded them from attempting, but which should be freely open to them. If a woman wishes to be a bricklayer, carpenter, painter or plasterer, she should have the same facilities as her brother for mastering the craft, under the same sort of social safeguards for health and just treatment as he enjoys. Work of all kinds must be done by the person of superior fitness for it. Occupations ought not be sexed. We used to hear of "gentlemen's" occupations, well-paid positions reserved for a few favored families. But Democracy broke down the barriers of those fat preserves and now, "The tools to him who can use them," is the industrial rule for men. Why should it not also be the rule for woman ? The right to work, the grim demand urged by the unemployed in times of depression, is now put forward in times of plenty and of want alike, by women; it should carry the right to wages for their work. Man has too often admitted woman's claim to an occupation only so long as it was unskilled and unpaid. Work she has ever had, and domestic drudgery, but fixed wages for her work have hitherto been seldom forthcoming. However, every census shows that in this respect conditions are improving and that an ever-multiplying number of women are entering upon lucrative occupations. But so far in manufactures they do not carry on exactly the same processes as men. We are so accustomed to see men and women artists, teachers, lawyers, authors, and doctors doing exactly the same kind of work that we are apt to forget that professional women form only a tiny fraction of the working women of the country. In the cotton and woolen mills, the clothing factories, the boot and shoe shops and the thousand and one smaller industries women are numbered by the ten thousand, while in the professions they are numbered by units. And in the shops and factories at present they usually have branches of work separate from the men's. When an economist recently tried to verify the oft-quoted statement that women receive less than men for the same work, he found it very difficult to discover cases in which they were doing exactly the same things. The lighter processes, requiring deftness rather than strength, go to them; the heavier processes to men. Of that natural division, at present, we make no complaint.

Woman's muscular development has been retarded by her forced adoption of an indoor life, her abstention from exercise and her exclusion from many occupations. But she is fast removing these disabilities. All efficient schools for girls provide gymnastic training; young women bicycle and walk, play tennis, golf and baseball; they have ceased to think it vulgar for them to be healthy; they are even adopting costumes suitable to their play and exercise. This natural procedure will strengthen their bodies in a generation or two and put them more nearly on equal terms with men.

Nobody can set limits to their physical improvement. Intelligent care and attention continued through the centuries will make them stronger and healthier than they have ever yet been, and prove their bodily equality with their brothers.

We ask only for a fair field and no favor, confident that, with equal chances, women will not in the long run prove inferior. Give men and women equal opportunities, and let them show in practice what work they are adapted to. Time is on the side of the women; the constant improvement of machinery reduces the area of industry reserved for the brute strength, which long centuries of habit have fostered in the men. It is that improvement which has favored the heavy recruiting in the army of women workers within the last few decades. And the process will certainly continue. No power can check Yankee inventiveness, and every invention is woman's ally, bringing nearer the day when muscular energy will give no advantage in industry.

Under those circumstances, what are the chief dangers and benefits? The benefits are plain. Women become independent beings, their economic freedom is a foundation for building individual character. Being no longer dependent upon father, brother, lover or husband, for a livelihood, they may develop their being in obedience to their own conscience. They are no longer merely appendages to another. Life may be free; love may be unbiased by sordid reasons. Marriage becomes a choice, not a necessity; love an exchange, not a purchase or sale. Spinsterhood and starvation cease to be synonymous. The excess of girls and women over boys and men, a million in Great Britain alone, and equally large in the "cotton towns" of New England and throughout the Eastern States, are no longer miserable drones, unable to marry under a monogamous law and yet forbidden to live by honest toil. Women become more self-respecting, and men's ideas about them more dignified. Both recede farther from the notions of the harem. Both begin to see new principles of life-long fellowship.

But the danger sare no less real.   They are the dangers which menace all prop-ertyless workers under our present *régime*, especially in the infancy of new indus-tries.   Just now, women are in about the same position with regard to the conditions of the employments they enter as men occupied in the middle of the century. They are crowding into new occupations and clamoring to the employers for work.   The supply of their labor, particularly in the unskilled grades, is in excess of the demands.   In bargaining as to wages and conditions they are individually at a hopeless disadvantage; with the result that their wages are low, their hours long and their work onerous.   As wage-earners, they must therefore use pre-cisely the same means of self-protection and advancement as men have success-fully employed.   These are of three classes:

1. They should grasp every chance to improve their skill.   They should seize the opportunities to increase their efficiency; not require these to be forced upon them.   When a woman who is a clerk has the chance to learn stenography and type-writing, she should eagerly take it, not make excuses and question her own ability to learn.   When new machines and new processes requiring greater skill and practice are introduced, women must show a willingness to give the neces-sary steady industry for mastering them.   Trade schools and technical classes must be thrown open and frequented by women as well as by men.   The hope of marriage must not be allowed to dull the industrial ambition and check the industrial effort.   So long as women are content in the sweating dens, the shirt, confectionery, india-rubber, white-lead, wall paper, garment, boot and shoe, and hosiery factories to do the least skilled work, and to do it as a stop-gap employ-ment, rather than a life's business, so long they will be ill paid and held indus-trially in low esteem.

2. For skilled and unskilled labor alike the next safeguard is essential—com-bination.   Women are slower than men to recognize that "union is strength." Leaders amongst them constantly deplore the difficulty of inducing them to stand together in enforcing their reasonable demands.   Consequently they some-times receive wages which their employer knows must be supplemented by the wages of sin.   Public protest and individual struggle by the workwomen are of little avail in these conditions.   Consider the position of a woman applying for employment in shop or factory.   At what unfair odds she stands.   Suppose she asks for a living wage and the employer offers a sum far below.   If she refuse his terms to her it means starvation.   She has no reserve to enable her to hold out.   A week's idleness means a week's hunger; possibly illness; probably the loss of her rented rooms.   But to the employer her refusal will cause the merest trifle of inconvenience, even if he can get nobody else at his own terms.   He will eat no morsel the less; his wife and children will still fare sumptuously; at the worst he will simply suffer a slight reduction of his output, an infinitesimal diminution of profit.   He can wait till hunger and misery have brought the recal-citrant woman to surrender.   Under these circumstances all that I said previously about freedom is a pitiful farce to the workwoman.   Opportunity to work for less than substinence wages is a mockery of freedom.   Real freedom demands not only the right to work, but the right to an ample living wage for the work.

Since in the nature of the case, isolated women and girls cannot exact that wage, like the men they must form unions, insist on collective bargaining, and stand united. Though the employer may dispense with any one of them, he cannot dispense with all. Acting as a unit they will put themselves more nearly on equal terms with him. At critical times the funds they have accumulated in the union will enable them to hold out for fair remuneration and their whole status will be improved. That woman may enter industrial life upon equal terms with men, nothing is more essential than that they shall learn like the men, to combine. Preferably they should be in a union along with the men who do the same kind of work, acting on the assumption that they will claim the same advantages and render the same services as their male colleagues.

3. Even unions, however, cannot enforce many of the conditions essential to the health of the worker of both sexes. and the well-being of society. They cannot insist successfully that all work places shall be properly ventilated, that machinery shall be safeguarded, that refuse gases shall be carried away by fans, that sanitary accommodation shall be provided for both sexes, and that meals shall not be eaten in unhealthy workrooms. Such matters must be enforced by legislative enactment.

Society has a special interest in enforcing them for women, because no dialectic can evade the fact that primarily upon the health of the women depends the stamina of the next generation. Women must have ready access to industry for the sake of their individual freedom and development. But the welfare of society must also be considered and is, indeed, paramount. In the interests of the community we must prevent the sacrifice of women in unregulated industry. Therein lies the chief danger in woman's entrance upon industrial occupations. If the hideous sacrifice of health and life which always occurs when competitive industry is unchecked were permitted for a few generations the whole nation would greatly suffer. Factory and workshop laws are, therefore, supremely necessary in regard to occupations in which women share. Such protective legislation really extends the freedom of the individual as well as preserves the strength of the community. Only five of the States prevent by law the over-working of adult women. In England, in the textile trades, where tens of thousands are employed, they have been saved from excessive hours for over thirty years; and in Quebec and Ontario, ten hours per day, or sixty hours per week, is now the legal maximum for adult women.

Similar laws should be passed in all the States or the waste of woman life may be terrible. While men are agitating for an eight-hour day, it surely is not too much to ask that women shall not work more than ten hours.

Ontario's sanitary regulations, which are better than those adopted by the States, may also be taken as a minimum for the protection of the health of the worker. They enact:

1. Every factory shall be kept in a cleanly state and free from effluvia arising from any source whatever.

2. Factories must not be overcrowded.

3. Proper ventilation must be furnished.

4. Suitable and separate closets and other conveniences must be provided for both sexes.

5. Machinery must be fenced and made safe for the worker.

Laundries, bakeshops and stores, as well as factories and workshops, come under the rules. These regulations should be enforced by a strong staff of factory inspectors, including women. Many complaints could not be made by women to men, that to a woman would eagerly be uttered. Inspectors are also more highly paid than the rank and file, an additional reason for insisting that women shall be amongst them.

Certain industries known to be deadly in their effects upon the workers, especially young girls, must be rigorously compelled to alter their methods until they are quite safe, no matter what additional money cost is involved. While we want young women to have equal opportunities with young men to learn manufacturing processes, we want neither to be deluded through ignorance, and forced by economic pressure, into situations where mutilation and death are more certain than on the battlefield.

Mr. Whiting in "No. 5 John Street," describes accurately one such factory in London, when he says "I see the hundreds of hands move wearily as they pass the gate, and I find that all but the quite fresh caught bear traces of this terrible toil. Theirs is an industry of which every stage of every operation costs a fraction of a life. They have all sorts of 'funny complaints.' Their eyes smart and water as they toil in the penetrating fumes, and they weep with the mechanical facility of experienced crocodiles. They see double at times, and the vast barn-like room swims round them as though its pots, brushes, garments, stuffs and furnace-fires of gas-jet were all but so much ruin in a whirlpool. Sometimes, as I learn in answer to inquiries, they 'ketch it in the lungs.' They invariably, as we have seen, 'ketch it in the knob' in the form of bilious headache. The moral effects are even more distressing. They lose their temper for nothing, and will find scope and verge enough for quarrel on a pin's point. Some have been known to go 'right off their chump,' and to be exceedingly rude to the overseers.

"Our factory, in truth, is a great spoiler of humanity, and especially of the weaker vessel. It seems to have the same destructive appetite for the latter as some monsters of fable. Their youth and freshness is but raw material, we turn them out as hags in no time—the manufactured article. Alas for their fleeting show of red and white."

"Ah, the pity of things marred—blossoms trampled by the hoofs of swine, girlhood cheated of its day. Some of them, like 'Nance,' bear it in silence, feeling that it is the price of keeping 'respectable.' Some snatch their beauty so to speak, out of the fire, and hurry with it to market for what it may still fetch as damaged ware. Others co-operate with the spoiler in his rage for results, and make for the dram-shop, as though they cannot keep their own nails from their own flesh." Such a description is painfully true of hundreds of factories in Europe and America. Since it is a medical fact that their effect is most deadly upon the women workers, they must be controlled out of existence, if necessary, rather than the hideous sacrifice of health and life be allowed to continue.

Whatever our opinion upon the question of equal suffrage, we are bound to admit that the wide employment of women industrially will of necessity be followed by their political enfranchisement. Working women whose conditions of labor are intimately affected by legislation will not be content to be shut out from opportunities to influence the lawmakers. Unenfranchised persons are not interesting to politicians. They only count votes. Therefore women who work will inevitably press to success the demands for full political rights, which they will go on to use for further amelioration of industrial conditions.

As the industrial employment of women extends, the collective regulation and control of industry must increase, for the greater the proportion of the population engaged in the shop and factory, the greater the necessity to see that conditions are just and progressive.

The thought and work for this progress should command the zeal of all citizens and especially of Christian people. Improvement is slow, only because so few citizens recognize their duty to the community. No religious work can be more potent for good than the moralization of industry; no sin of omission is more harmful than the neglect of our duty to the State.

With patient study and unwearying ardor the community must mould its arrangements, until to every woman and every man alike there is guaranteed an opportunity, with reasonable exertion, and under pleasant conditions, to earn a generous livelihood.

Lightning Source UK Ltd.
Milton Keynes UK
UKHW020347081118
331957UK00008B/154/P